PIANO · VOCAL · GUITAR

T0088355

EGYPT STATION

PAUL McCARTNEY

Album artwork based upon 'Egypt Station' and 'Egypt Station II' paintings by Paul McCartney
Art Direction and Design: Gary Card and Ferry Gouw
Egypt Station track logo and conceptional ideas: Rebecca and Mike
© MPL Communications Inc.

ISBN: 978-1-5400-4302-3

 MPL COMMUNICATIONS, INC.
http://mplcommunications.com

HAL·LEONARD®

Visit Hal Leonard Online at
www.halleonard.com

Contact Us:
Hal Leonard
7777 West Bluemound Road
Milwaukee, WI 53213
Email: info@halleonard.com

In Europe contact:
Hal Leonard Europe Limited
42 Wigmore Street
Marylebone, London, W1U 2RN
Email: info@halleonardeurope.com

In Australia contact:
Hal Leonard Australia Pty. Ltd.
4 Lentara Court
Cheltenham, Victoria, 3192 Australia
Email: info@halleonard.com.au

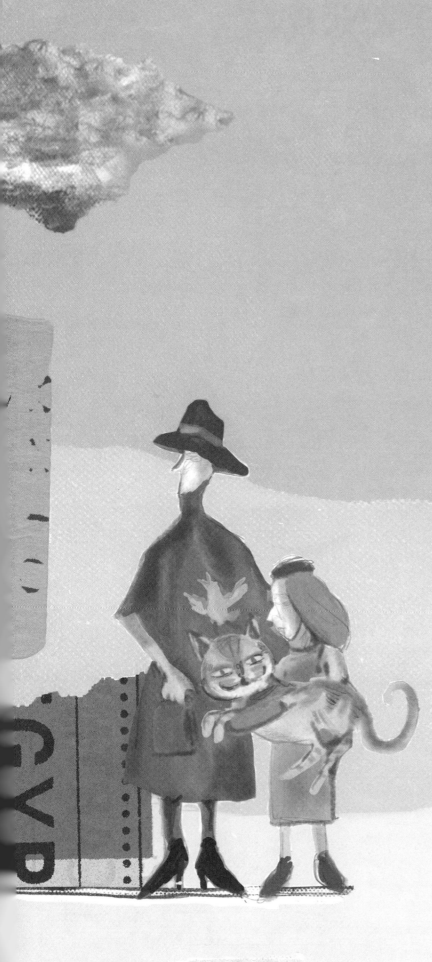

I DON'T KNOW

Words and Music by
PAUL McCARTNEY

COME ON TO ME

Words and Music by
PAUL McCARTNEY

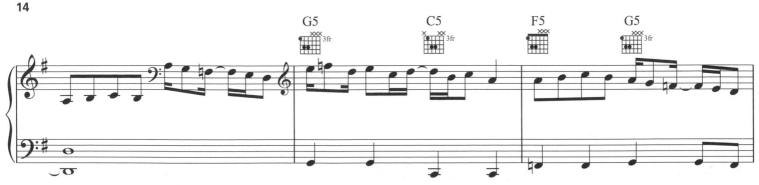

Well, ___ I saw you flash a smile ___

___ come on ___ to you.   If you come on to me, ___

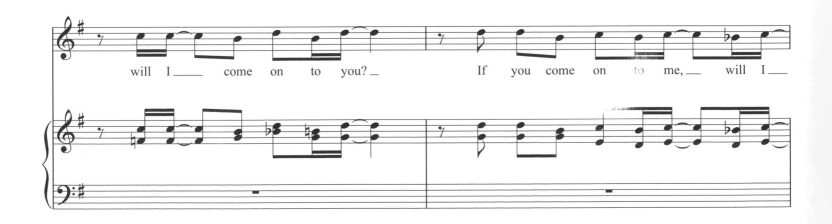

will I ___ come on to you? ___   If you come on to me, ___ will I ___

HAPPY WITH YOU

Words and Music by
PAUL McCARTNEY

lots of good things __ to do, _____ oh, yeah. __

Like
hear the high clear rob - in sing, __
Throw a pock - et full of coins __

walk a blue - bell car - pet.
in the Trev - i Foun - tain.
Watch the chil - dren play - ing games, __
See an ice - cold run - ning stream __

20

WHO CARES

Words and Music by
PAUL McCARTNEY

Moderately fast

Did you ev-er get hurt by the words peo-ple say ___ and the
ev-er get lost in the heart of a crowd and the

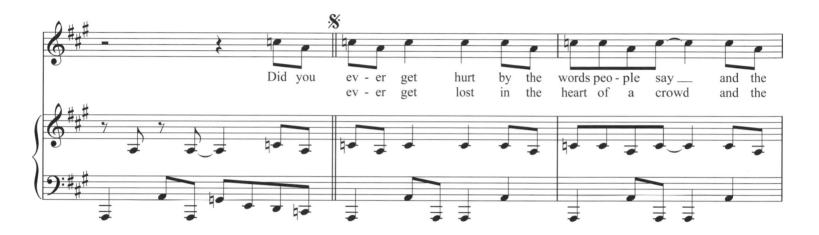

things that they do ___ when they're pick-in' on you? ___
peo-ple a-round keep ___ push-ing you down? ___

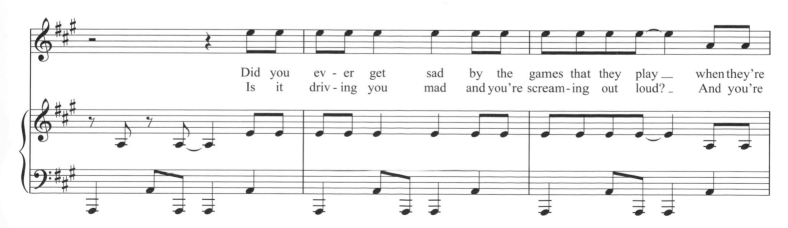

Did you ev-er get sad by the games that they play ___ when they're
Is it driv-ing you mad and you're scream-ing out loud? ___ And you're

Who cares a-bout the pain in your heart? _ Who

cares a-bout you? _____ I do. _____

You've been left _____ in the rain. _____

FUH YOU

Words and Music by PAUL McCARTNEY
and RYAN TEDDER

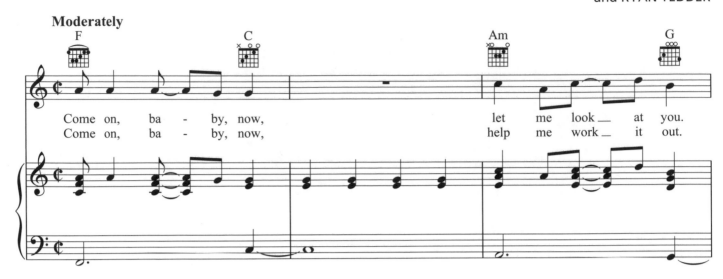

Come on, ba - by, now, let me look __ at you.
Come on, ba - by, now, help me work __ it out.

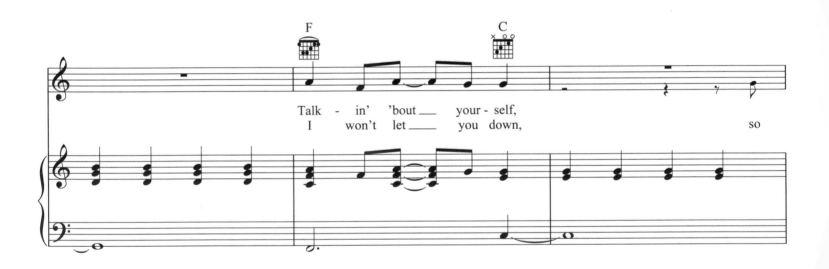

Talk - in' 'bout __ your - self,
I won't let __ you down, so

try to tell __ the truth.
you don't need __ to shout.

I could stay up half __ the night,
I could stay up half __ the night,

CONFIDANTE

Words and Music by
PAUL McCARTNEY

Acoustic Folk

mf

You used to be my con - fi - dante, _

my un - der - neath the stair - case friend. _ But I fell out of

love with you _ and brought our _ ro - mance to an end. _

CAESAR ROCK

Words and Music by
PAUL McCARTNEY

To Coda ⊕

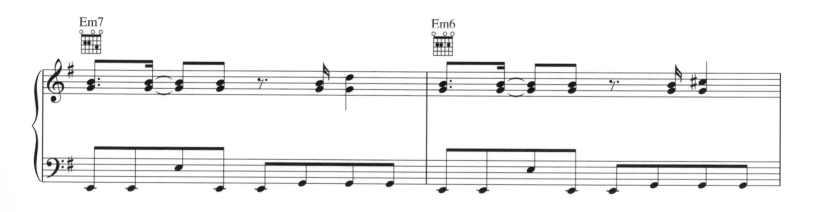

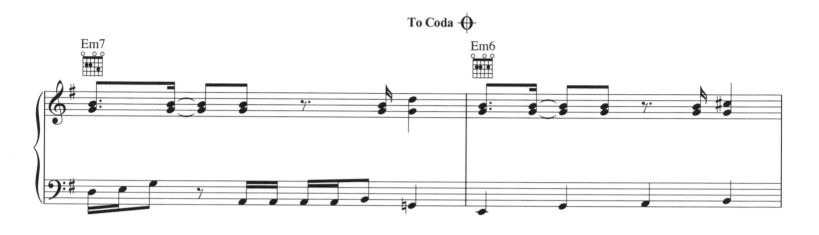

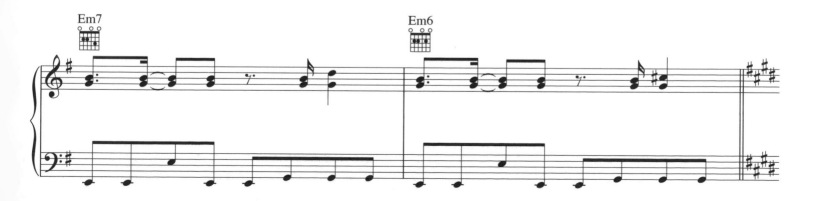

PEOPLE WANT PEACE

Words and Music by
PAUL McCARTNEY

Lad-ies and gen-tle men, stand-ing be-fore _ you with some-thing im-por-tant to say. _ With some tre-pe-da-tion I crave your at-ten-tion but I'm not gon-na let an-y-thing get in my way. _ The mes-sage is sim-ple, it's straight from the heart _ and I know _

Peo - ple want peace. ____

Peo - ple want peace. ____

HAND IN HAND

Words and Music by
PAUL McCARTNEY

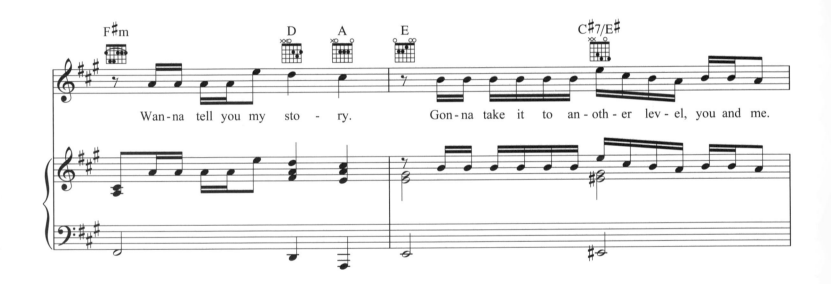

DOMINOES

Words and Music by
PAUL McCARTNEY

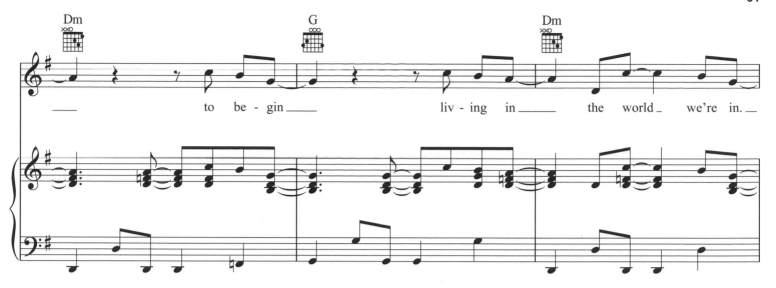

to be-gin ___ liv-ing in ___ the world ___ we're in. ___

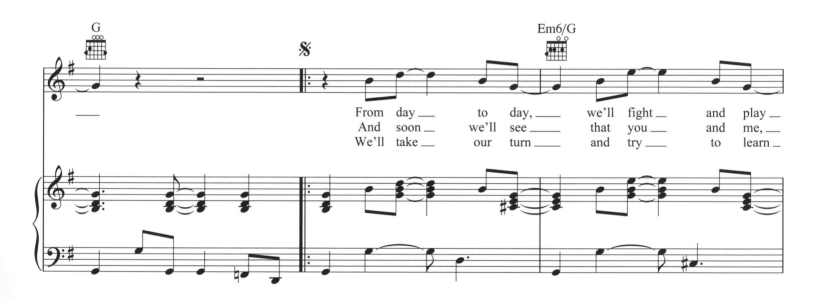

From day ___ to day, ___ we'll fight ___ and play ___
And soon ___ we'll see ___ that you ___ and me, ___
We'll take ___ our turn ___ and try ___ to learn ___

for what ___ we need. ___ We'll soon ___ for-get ___
we're real - ly friends. ___ We broke ___ the code ___
to sing ___ and dance. ___ We'll hedge ___ our bets ___

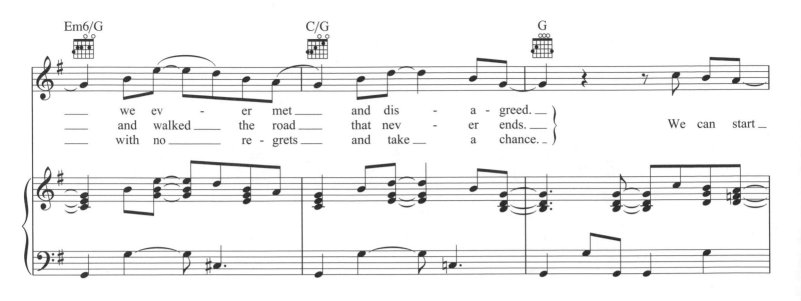

we ev - er met ___ and dis - a - greed. ___
and walked ___ the road ___ that nev - er ends. ___
with no ___ re - grets ___ and take ___ a chance. ___
We can start ___

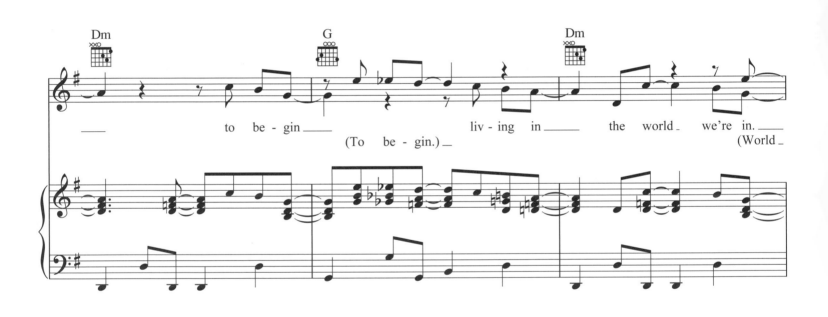

to be - gin ___ liv - ing in ___ the world ___ we're in. ___
(To be - gin.) ___ (World ___

This is it, ___ here and now. ___ We can find ___
___ we're in.) ___ (This is it.) ___ (Here and now.)

In time _ we'll know, _ it's all _ a show, _ it's been _ a blast. _

BACK IN BRAZIL

Words and Music by
PAUL McCARTNEY

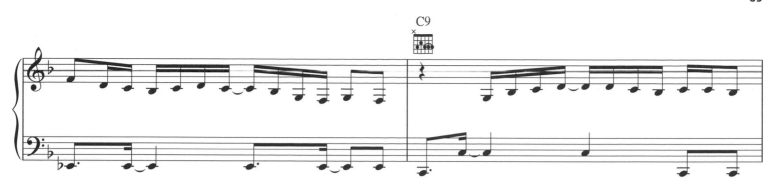

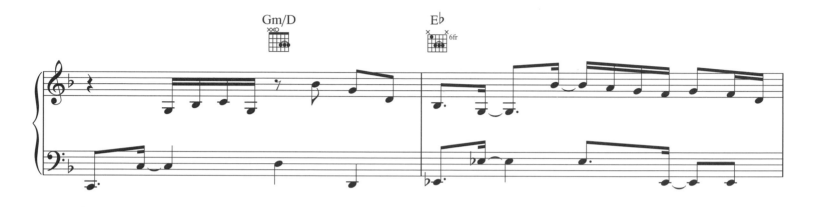

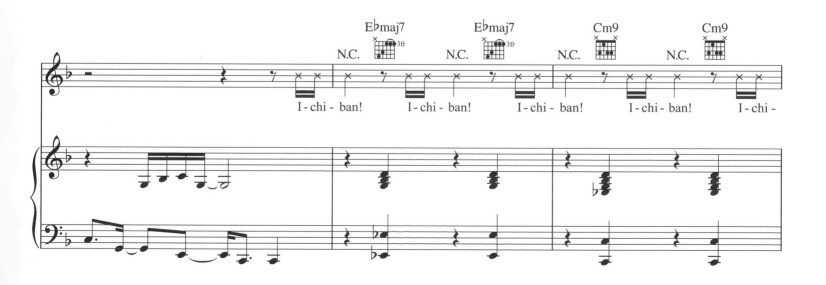

I - chi - ban!   I - chi - ban!   I - chi - ban!   I - chi - ban!   I - chi -

So we raise a fam - ily as the clouds roll by,

mak - ing pic - tures of us in the sky. The kids are hap - py and they don't ask why.

Ba ba ba ___ ba ba, you and I.

DO IT NOW

Words and Music by
PAUL McCARTNEY

Moderate Ballad

Got the time, the in-cli-na-tion. I have
gret the steps I'm tak-ing, the de-

an-swered your in-vi-ta-tion. I'll be leav-ing in the morn-
ci-sion that I'm mak-ing is the right one or I'm nev-

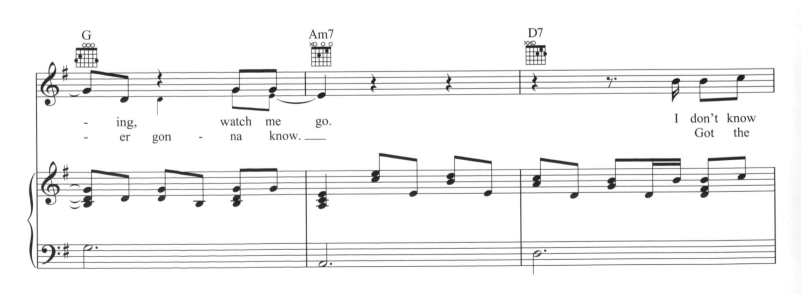

-ing, watch me go. I don't know
-er gon-na know. Got the

DESPITE REPEATED WARNINGS

Words and Music by
PAUL McCARTNEY

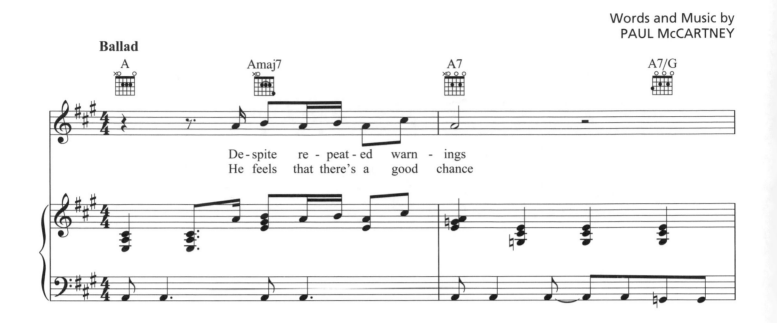

De - spite re - peat - ed warn - ings
He feels that there's a good chance

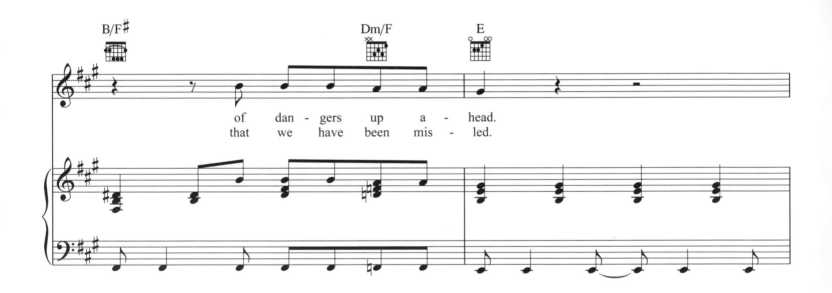

of dan - gers up a - head.
that we have been mis - led.

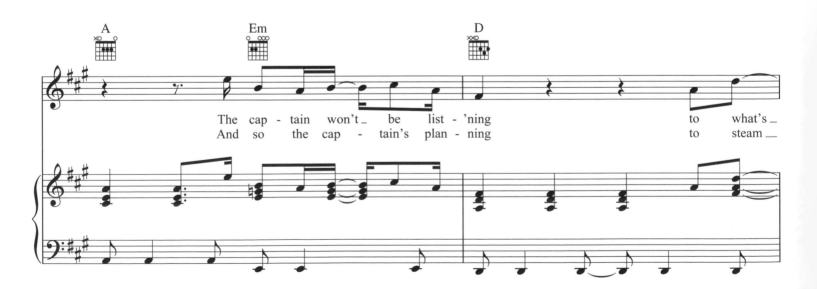

The cap - tain won't_ be list - 'ning   to what's_
And so the cap - tain's plan - ning   to steam_

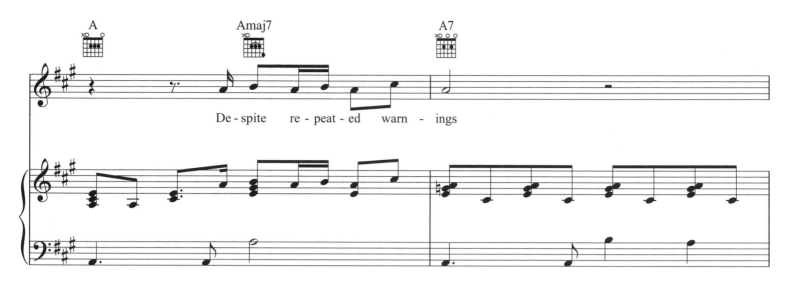

De - spite re - peat - ed warn - ings

of dan - gers up a - head.

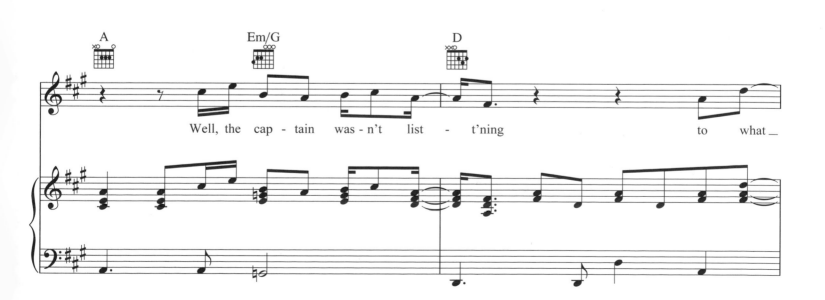

Well, the cap - tain was - n't list - t'ning to what

was said. _____

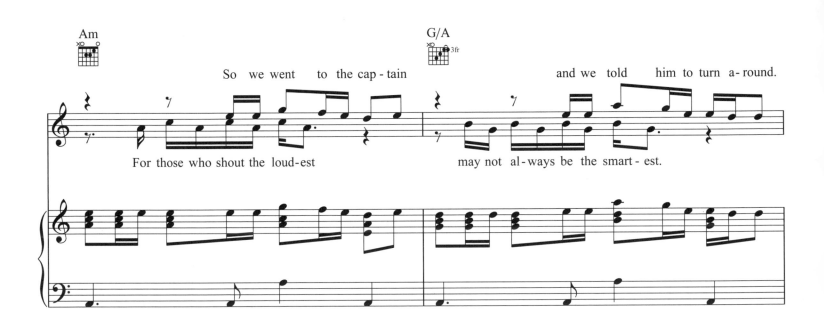

So we went to the cap - tain and we told him to turn a - round.

For those who shout the loud-est may not al - ways be the smart - est.

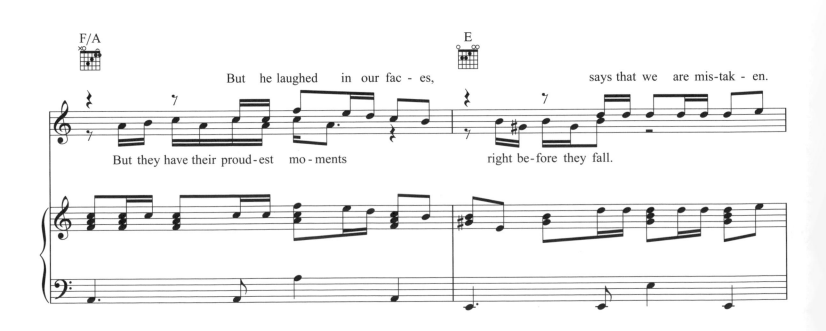

But he laughed in our fac - es, says that we are mis-tak - en.

But they have their proud-est mo - ments right be-fore they fall.

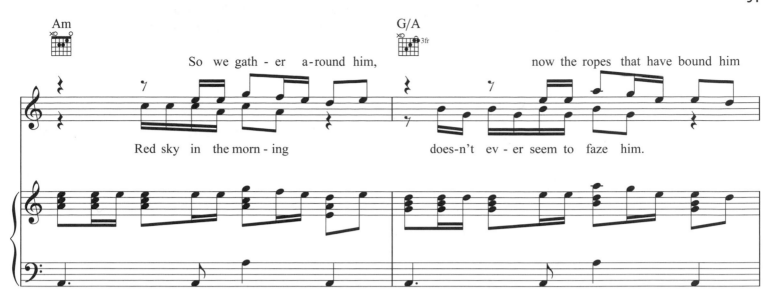

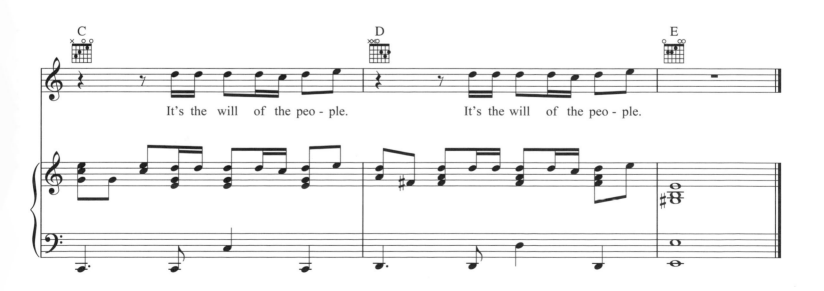

HUNT YOU DOWN/NAKED/C-LINK

Words and Music by
PAUL McCARTNEY

Moderately fast

I can't find my love _____ no mat-ter how hard _____ I try. _____
trav-'lin' 'round the world, _____ try'n' to find a per-fect mate. _____

Much slower

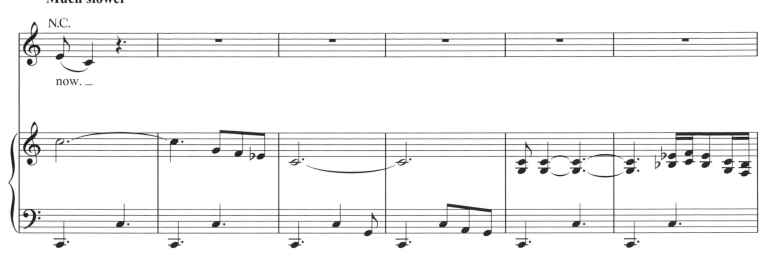

now. __

8vb -

(8vb) - |

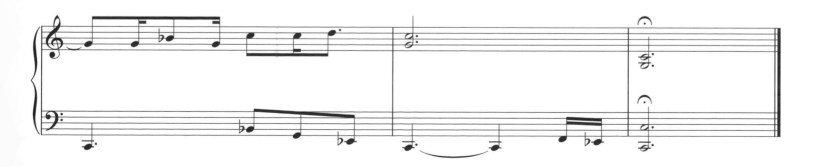